20 Forex Scalping Trading Strategies
By Thomas Carter

ISBN-13: 978-1508429401
ISBN-10: 1508429405

I0484746

DISCLAIMER

Trading forex and other on-exchange and over-the-counter products carries a high level of risk and may not be suitable for all investors. The high degree of leverage associated with such trading can result in losses, as well as gains. the past performance of any trading strategy or methodology is not indicative of future results, which can vary due to market volatility; it should not be interpreted as a forecast of future performance You should carefully consider whether such trading is suitable for you in light of your financial condition, level of experience and appetite for risk and seek advice from independent financial adviser, if you have any doubts.

Table of Contents

What Is Forex Scalping ?

Fores scalping is a trading strategy used by forex traders to buy or sell a currency pair and then hold it for a short period of time in an attempt to make a profit. A forex scalper looks to make some number of trades and earn a small profit each time.

The name "Forex Scalping" sounds risky. But the scalping method can be low risk when they implemented during the best times for scalping in the market. Many new forex traders attempt to scalp the market during times of volatility or of news trading, but these highly volatile trading times are risky for all trading strategies, including the forex scalping strategy.

The trader must always determine ahead of time their risk management strategy. The Forex Scalping trader must decide to get out of bad trades when they have lower pip losses. Waiting for a hopeful recovery if the very short trade does not go as expected is too dangerous. It is best to take profits of small pips and also limit amount of pips accepted as loss. Otherwise one larger bad trade could completely wipe out numerous smaller profitable trades.

This book will help you in choosing the best forex scalping strategies that work for you.

Scalping Forex Strategy # 1

Time Frame:

1 min

Pairs:

Major Currency Pairs

Indicators:

Bollinger Bands (20,2)

ADX (14)

RSI (7)

Long Entry:

Price to move below the lower Bollinger Bands, RSI above the 30 line and ADX < 32 at the same time.

Short Entry:

Price to move above the upper Bollinger Bands, RSI below the 70 line and ADX < 32 at the same time.

Target Profit:

Exit position when the price touches the middle band or 6 pips fix target profit.

Stop Loss:

Stop loss on high / low entry bar or 7 pips loss.

Scalping Forex Strategy # 2

Time Frame:

1 min

Pairs:

EUR/USD, GBP/USD, AUD/USD

Indicators:

50 EMA

100 EMA

Stochastic (5,3,3)

Long Entry:

- 50 EMA > 100 EMA
- Find significant level of support.
- Wait for the currency price to retreat back to the support line.
- Wait for the stochastic oscillator to trade from below 20 back above 20.
- Open a long trade.
- Place stop loss 3 pips below support.
- Profit target should be at least 7-12 pips.

Short Entry:

- 50 EMA < 100 EMA
- Find significant level of resistance.
- Wait for the currency price to retreat back to the resistance line.
- Wait for the stochastic oscillator to trade from above 80 back below 80.

- Open a short trade.
- Place stop loss 3 pips above resistance.
- Profit target should be at least 7-12 pips.

Scalping Forex Strategy # 3

Time Frame:

5 min

Pairs:

EUR/USD, GBP/USD, AUD/USD

Indicators:

Parabolic SAR (0.01-0.01)

MACD (64,128,9)

100 EMA

Long Entry:

When the price is above the EMA 100 and Parabolic SAR dot is up and MACD > 0

Short Entry:

When the price is below the EMA 100 and the Parabolic SAR dot is down and MACD < 0

Stop Loss:

3 pips below or above the first Parabolic SAR dot.

Take Profit:

Price objective is 7-12 pips.

Scalping Forex Strategy # 4

Time Frame:

1 min

Pairs:

EUR/USD, GBP/USD, AUD/USD

Indicators:

EMA 50 High

EMA 50 Low

EMA 50 Close

EMA 100 close

Stochastic (14,3,3)

Long Entry:

Buy Zone: EMA's band > 100 EMA

We wait for a rally back toward the EMA's band (EMA 50 High, Low and Close) for the best possible entry. The stochastic oscillator is oversold, value +30 when crosses towards up.

Short Entry:

Sell Zone: EMA's band < 100 EMA

We wait for a rally back toward the EMA's band (EMA 50 High, Low and Close) for the best possible entry. The stochastic oscillator is overbought, value +70 when crosses towards down.

Stop Loss:

Place stop loss 3 pips below or above the upper or lower 50 EMA.

Take Profit:

Price objective is 7-12 pips.

Scalping Forex Strategy # 5

Time Frame:

1 min or 5 min (choose one)

Pairs:

EUR/USD, AUD/USD, GBP/USD

Indicators:

50 SMA for 1 min TF

21 SMA for 5 min TF

CCI (45)

Parabolic SAR (0.02, 0.2)

Long Entry:

When Parabolic SAR dot > SMA and CCI (45) > 100

Short Entry:

When Parabolic SAR dot < SMA and CCI (45) < -100

Stop Loss:

Place stop loss on the SMA.

Profit Target:

EUR/USD: 7-12 pips

AUD/USD: 5-8 pips

GBP/USD: 7-15 pips

Scalping Forex Strategy # 6

Time Frame: 5min

Pairs:

EUR/USD, AUD/USD, GBP/USD

Indicators:

Fractal

6 EMA

12 EMA

34 EMA

Long Entry:

6 EMA is higher than 12 EMA which is higher than 34 EMA.

The Up Fractal need to be form above the EMAs for long.

Open a buy trade when the price is higher than the Up Fractal by 2 pips.

Short Entry:

6 EMA is less than 12 EMA which is less than 34 EMA.

The Down Fractal need to form below the EMAs for short.

Open a short trade when the price is lower than the Down Fractal by 2 pips.

Stop Loss:

Set the stop loss just below the previous up fractal for short trades or just below the down fractal for a long trade.

Take Profit:

AUD/USD: 6 pips

EUR/USD: 8 pips

GBP/USD: 10 pips

Scalping Forex Strategy # 7

Time Frame:

5 min

Pairs:

EUR/USD

Indicators:

MACD (12,26,1)

Stochastic (5,3,3)

EMA 5 to the close

EMA 5 to the open

Buy Signal:

- When the stochastic crosses up from the 20 line and is not overbought.
- The MACD closses higher than the previous time interval.
- The signal candle closses higher and bullish.
- The 5 EMA to the close has crossed the 5 EMA to the open.
- Stop Loss → the low of the previous candle or 20 pips.
- Take Profit → close when the 5 EMA to the close has crossed the 5 EMA to the open.

Sell Signal:

- When the stochastic crosses down from the 80 line and is not oversold.
- The MACD closses lower than the previous time interval.
- The signal candle closses lower and bearish.
- The 5 EMA to the close has crosses the 5 EMA to the open.

- Stop Loss → the high of the previous candle or 20 pips.
- Take Profit → close when the 5 EMA to the close has crossed the 5 EMA to the open.

Charts:

Look at my blog: thomascarterbook.blogspot.com

Scalping Forex Strategy # 8

Time Frame:

5 min

Pairs:

EUR/USD, GBP/USD

Indicators:

10 EMA

50 EMA

Bollinger Bands (30,2)

Parabolic SAR (0.03, 0.2)

RSI (14) (Buy level 60, Sell level 40)

MACD (12,26,9)

Long Entry:

- When the price of the closed candle breaks upper Bollinger Bands
- 10 EMA > 50 EMA
- RSI (14) > 60
- MACD > 0

Short Entry:

- When the price of the closed candle breaks lower Bollinger Bands
- 10 EMA < 50 EMA
- RSI (14) < 40
- MACD < 0

Stop Loss:

Recent swing high / low or 10 – 15 pips.

Exit:

When the Parabolic SAR change direction or

EUR/USD = 7 pips

GBP/USD = 9 pips

Scalping Forex Strategy # 9

Time Frame:

5 min

Pairs:

EUR/USD, AUD/USD, GBP/USD

Indicators:

Bollinger Bands (20,2)

Money Flow Index (8)

Long Entry:

When the Money Flow Index is in overbought, the price close outside the lower Bollinger Bands. Wait for bullish candle.

Short Entry:

When the Money Flow Index is in oversold, the price close outside the upper Bollinger Bands. Wait for bearish candle.

Stop Loss:

Place stop loss on the upper or lower Bollinger Bands

Profit Target:

AUD/USD = 6 pips

EUR/USD = 8 pips

GBP/USD = 10 pips

Scalping Forex Strategy # 10

Time Frame:

5 min

Pairs:

EUR/USD, AUD/USD, GBP/USD

Indicators:

Candlestick

Entry:

3 consecutive candlestick must be either bullish or bearish. Also it must be in slope.

Stop Loss:

Higher or Lower second candle from 3 consecutive candlestick.

Profit Target:

AUD/USD = 6 pips

EUR/USD = 8 pips

GBP/USD = 10 pips

Scalping Forex Strategy # 11

Time Frame:

1 min and 5 min

Pairs:

EUR/USD

Indicators:

Bollinger Bands (20,2)

Long Trades:

The price should be outside the lower Bollinger Bands on 1 min chart.

When the price has extended by 7/10 pips below the lower band on 1 min chart and 5 min chart is also showing the price outside the lower Bollinger Bands go long.

Place stop loss 10 pips below the entry point.

When in the trade as soon as you are showing 10/15 pips profit exit the trade.

A secondary entry can be taken if the price moves 15 pips below your first entry stopping you out. If this second position is stopped out do not trade this again, wait for another opportunity.

Short Trades:

The price should be outside the upper Bollinger Bands on 1 min chart.

When the price has extended by 7/10 pips above the upper band on 1 min chart and 5 min chart is also showing the price outside the upper Bollinger Bands go short.

Place stop loss 10 pips above the entry point.

When in the trade as soon as you are showing 10/15 pips profit exit the trade.

A secondary entry can be taken if the price moves 15 pips above your first entry stopping you out. If this second position is stopped out do not trade this again, wait for another opportunity.

Scalping Forex Strategy # 12

Time Frame: 1min

Pairs:

GBP/USD

Indicators:

10 EMA

21 EMA

50 EMA

MACD (3,5,3)

Long Trade:

10 EMA > 21 EMA > 50 EMA

The yellow MACD line go to below 0 and then come back up above the 0 level.

When the bar closes that cause the yellow MACD to close above 0 then we enter our long position on the close of the bar (or open of the next bar).

Short Trade:

10 EMA < 21 EMA < 50 EMA

The yellow MACD line go to above 0 and then come back down below the 0 level

When the bar closes that cause the yellow MACD to close below 0then we enter our short position on the close of the bar (or open of the next bar).

Exit Strategy and Stop Loss:

Place stop loss above or below previous bar and move your stop loss up or down as each new bar is formed.

Charts: Look at my blog: thomascarterbook.blogspot.com

Scalping Forex Strategy # 13

Time Frame:

5 min or 15 min (choose one)

Pairs:

EUR/USD, AUD/USD, GBP/USD

Indicators:

Real MACD Colored (12,26,1)

Stochastic (14,3,3)

6 EMA Smoothed

4 EMA

Long Entry:

- When the stochastic crosses up from the 20 line and is not overbought.
- The MACD > 0
- The 4 EMA has crossed up the 6 EMA Smoothed.
- Stochastic > 50

Short Entry:

- When the stochastic crosses down from the 80 line and is not oversold.
- The MACD < 0
- The 4 EMA has crossed down the 6 EMA Smoothed.
- Stochastic < 50

Stop Loss:

The low / high of the previous candlestick.

Take profit for 5 min TF:

EUR/USD = 8 pip

AUD/USD = 6 pip

GBP/USD = 10 pip

Take Profit for 15 min TF:

EUR/USD = 12 pip

AUD/USD = 9 pip

GBP/USD = 15 pip

Scalping Forex Strategy # 14

Time Frame:

1 min

Pairs:

EUR/USD

Indicators:

10 EMA

Bollinger Bands (18,2)

Parabolic SAR (0.018, 0.08)

MACD (12,26,9)

RSI (14)

Buy Setup:

- 10 EMA crosses above middle of Bollinger Bands
- MACD is above zero line
- RSI > 50
- Use Parabolic SAR only as visual trend direction aid

Sell Setup:

- 10 EMA crosses below middle of Bollinger Bands
- MACD is below zero line
- RSI < 50
- Use Parabolic SAR only as a visual trend direction aid

Stop Loss:

10 pips

Take Profit: 7 -12 pips

Scalping Forex Strategy # 15

Time Frame:

1 min

Pairs:

EUR/USD

Indicators:

Bollinger Bands (18,1)

3 EMA

MACD (12,26,1)

RSI (14)

Long Entry:

3 EMA crossed above middle Bollinger Bands

RSI > 50

MACD > 0

Short Entry:

3 EMA crossed below middle Bollinger Bands

RSI < 50

MACD < 0

Stop Loss:

4 pips below or above middle Bollinger Bands

Take Profit:

7 – 12 pips

Scalping Forex Strategy # 16

Time Frame:

5 min

Pairs:

EUR/USD, GBP/USD, AUD/USD

Indicators:

Parabolic SAR (0.011, 0.11) – on the chart

8 SMA – on the chart

MACD (5,8,9) and Parabolic SAR (0.01, 0.1) – on this MACD

Long Entry:

When the price is greater than 8 SMA and the two Parabolic SAR are in agreement.

Short Entry:

When the price is less than 8 SMA and the two Parabolic SAR are in agreement.

Stop Loss:

Previous swing low / high or max 12 pips

Profit Target:

EUR/USD = 8 pips

AUD/USD = 6 pips

GBP/USD = 10 pips

Scalping Forex Strategy # 17

Time Frame:

5 min

Pairs:

EUR/USD, GBP/USD, AUD/USD

Indicators:

EMA 16

EMA 48

Laguerre

Long Entry Rules:

- The closing price is stay above the EMA 16
- The EMA 16 stays above the EMA 48
- Laguerre cuts above 0.8 level
- Stop Loss = 30 pips from entry point
- Take profit half of your position when price has gone above 20 pips
- Take profit the rest when the EMA 16 cuts below EMA 48 and closing price stays below the EMA 48

Short Entry Rules:

- The closing price is stay below the EMA 16
- The EMA 16 stays below the EMA 48
- Laguerre cuts below 0.2 level
- Stop Loss = 30 pips from entry point
- Take profit half of your position when the price has gone below 20 pips

- Take profit of the rest when the EMA 16 cuts above EMA 48 and closing price stays above the EMA 48

Scalping Forex Strategy # 18

Time Frame:

5 min

Pairs:

Major Currency Pairs

Indicators:

Zig Zag (28,5,3)

MACD (21,89,1)

CCI (34)

CCI (46)

Long Trade Rules:

- The zig-zag has formed a low swing point
- Both the CCI 34 and CCI 46 cross the 0 line from below
- MACD > 0
- You could also enter long when both the CCI 34 and CCI 46 cross the 100 level if condition 1-3 are met. Usually this produces stronger signals.
- Aim to take profit of no more than 5 pips
- Exit when you met your profit target or when the swing point of the zig zag is high (whichever comes first)

Short Trade Rules:

- The zig-zag has formed a high swing point
- Both the CCI 34 and CCI 46 cross the 0 line from above
- MACD < 0
- You could also enter short when both CCI 34 and CCI 46

cross the -100 level if condition 1-3 are met. Usually this produces stronger signals.

– Aim to take profit of no more than 5 pips

– Exit when you met your profit target or when the swing point of the zig zag is low (whichever comes first)

Charts:

Look at my blog: thomascarterbook.blogspot.com

Chart Explanation (5 min EUR/USD):

1. Low swing point of zig-zag

2. MACD > 0

3. CCI 34 and CCI 46 cross 0 from below and later crossed 100 from below. The cross of either 0 from below or 100 from below or the cross of both 0 and 100 is needed for a long trade.

4. Enter long at 1.49515

5. Take profit at 1.49560

Scalping Forex Strategy # 19

Time Frame:

5 min

Pairs:

EUR/USD, AUD/USD, GBP/USD

Indicators:

ADX(14)

5 EMA

15 EMA

30 EMA

Stochastic (5,3,3)

Long Entry:

ADX > 20

15 EMA > 30 EMA

5 EMA > 15 EMA

Stochastic > 50 (if the trending is up re-entry when stochastic re-crosses up 50 level from the bottom)

Short Entry:

ADX > 20

15 EMA < 30 EMA

5 EMA < 15 EMA

Stochastic < 50 (if the trending is down re-entry when the stochastic re-crosses down 50 level from above)

Stop Loss:

10 pips

Profit Target:

AUD/USD = 5 pips

EUR/USD = 7 pips

GBP/USD = 9 pips

Scalping Forex Strategy # 20

Time Frame:

1 min

Pairs:

EUR/USD, AUD/USD, GBP/USD

Indicators:

230 EMA

115 EMA

46 EMA

23 EMA

Stochastic (3,2,2)

Long Entry Rules:

- 115 EMA must be above the 230 EMA
- 23 EMA must be above the 46 EMA
- 23/46 EMA must also be above the 115/230 EMA
- Stochastic go below the 30 level and then back above the 30 level

Short Entry Rules:

- 115 EMA must be below the 230 EMA
- 23 EMA must be below the 46 EMA
- 23/46 EMA must also be below the 115/230 EMA
- Stochastic go above the 70 level and then back below the 70 level

Stop Loss:

3 pips above or below 46 EMA

Profit Target:

AUD/USD = 6 pips

EUR/USD = 8 pips

GBP/USD = 10 pips

FINAL WORDS

Thank you for downloading this book. I hope this book was able to help you to jump start your forex trading adventure. If you enjoyed this book, please take the time to share your thoughts and post a review on amazon. It's be greatly appreciated !

I wish you all the best with trading,

Thomas Carter

RECOMMENDED READING

Go ahead and check out the other great books by Thomas Carter !

Forex Made Simple: 20 Forex Trading Strategy (A Step-By-Step Trading Strategy For 1 Hour Time frame)

17 Forex Trading Strategies Collection (4H and Daily Time Frame)

20 Forex Trading Strategies (5 Minute Time Frame)

Forex Trend Following Strategies: How To Make Big Gain With Low Risk Currency Trading

Bollinger Band Trading Systems: Step-By-Step 7 Profitable Forex Trading Strategies

Golden Trading System: 5 Solid Step-By-Step Forex Trading Strategies

www.ingramcontent.com/pod-product-compliance
Lightning Source LLC
Chambersburg PA
CBHW072314200526
45168CB00014B/1569